STEPPING
INSIDE THE
GATE

DR. DANNY L. MOODY

WESTBOW
PRESS®
A DIVISION OF THOMAS NELSON
& ZONDERVAN

WestBow Press books may be ordered through booksellers or by contacting:

WestBow Press
A Division of Thomas Nelson & Zondervan
1663 Liberty Drive
Bloomington, IN 47403
www.westbowpress.com
844-714-3454

Scripture taken from the King James Version of the Bible.

ISBN: 978-1-6642-8674-0 (sc)
ISBN: 978-1-6642-8672-6 (hc)
ISBN: 978-1-6642-8673-3 (e)

Library of Congress Control Number: 2022923154

Print information available on the last page.

WestBow Press rev. date: 12/19/2022

CONTENTS

FOREWORD

Danny Moody has taken a step inside the gate of death in the pages you are about to read. Most believers have some concept of what happens when we die and move into God's eternity. However, while we are mourning the loss of one we love, what has really happened to that individual? What was this person's journey from this life into eternity like? What was it like when the earthly body transformed into what the person will become with the Lord? What really happened in *that miraculous moment*? That time is fraught with mystery. When the body dies, the real person is now a living soul/spirit. We cannot imagine a bodiless person who cannot be seen. All believers who die wait for the resurrection before they will ever have new bodies. The mystery of that reality is staggering. We have no point of reference for a bodiless soul/spirit. It is both mind-boggling and soul searching.

Read these pages and Danny Moody will help you understand what it means to be *Stepping Inside the Gate*. One thing is for sure: God has prepared His people for that *miraculous moment* between *now* and *then*. These pages will bring better understanding of that time when the gate of death is opened. It will be, also, a strong encouragement for those who have not yet found Jesus Christ as their Savior to move forward in faith to receive the eternal life He has provided.

Jimmy Draper
President Emeritus, LifeWay

INTRODUCTION

"He's gone!"

A gasp slips from the lips of his daughter on the other side of the bed, holding tightly to his hand. A sob is heard from his wife of fifty-three years as she buries her face in the tear-soaked handkerchief in her hand. His younger sister must take a seat in the bedside chair as a precaution against the trembling that she feels in her legs.

The hours spent at his bedside, caring for him, speaking softly to him, and doing everything possible to keep him comfortable have now come to an end. The constant humming and chugging of the oxygen concentrator that has filled the room for weeks can now be silenced. No one is speaking, only staring at the now lifeless body of the man who has been so central to nearly every aspect of their lives. Now, he's gone.

We all know that this moment is coming. How do we ever really prepare for this sixty-second period where we wait to see if the person will take just one more breath? Then, the person doesn't, and he or she is gone.

What has happened? What has *really* happened?

We who are standing by the bed and still have the breath of life in our lungs might simply say that the person has "passed away" or has "gone to be with Jesus" or has "entered heaven."

For us, a series of events now begins. We must call the hospice personnel. We must contact the preferred funeral home. We must make the phone calls to let loved ones know that he or she is no longer with us. We must make travel arrangements for out-of-town family members. We must start the dreaded process of preparing for a funeral or memorial service.

We all have our own verbal version of what we have just seen and experienced, and that story will be told repeatedly over the next few days. We all know the tasks that now lie before us. For us, what has just transpired means a gamut of emotions to deal with, responsibilities to shoulder, plans to make, and people to interact with.

For us, what has just happened means all these things and much more. But *wait! What about the person who has died?* What just happened from *his or her* vantage point? We watched; we saw; we felt; we grieve. But what about the deceased? May I ask again with even more emphasis? What *really* happened here from the deceased person's point of view?

The scenario that we have just described happens

thousands of times a day with variations of times, places, genders, family members, and causes of death. Some deaths take place in hospitals, some in homes, some in nursing homes, some at accident sites, and the list goes on.

Up until now, and encompassing all human history, there have been only two individuals who left this world without dying: Enoch (Genesis 5:24) and Elijah (2 Kings 2:11). Unless Jesus comes to take us home to be with Him in the Rapture, every one of us will one day take our final breaths in this world and *be gone*.

I have had the privilege of serving in full-time ministry for forty years. Most of that time has included serving as a senior pastor of a local church. I count that as a supreme and blessed privilege that God has seen fit to allow me. During that time, I have stood beside many beds as individuals draw their last breaths and depart this life. Those experiences, especially those where the departing loved one was a believer in Jesus Christ, have made it clear that at that moment something happens that we who are standing by cannot see. I am speaking of that moment, that split-second, when life on earth ends. I call this *that miraculous moment*. The stories I could tell are plentiful, and the experiences are life-altering. The promises of the Scriptures concerning the death and dying of the saint of God have unfolded right before my eyes. It is truly a *miraculous moment*.

If you picked up this book to read about accounts of

individuals who have had near-death experiences and have come back to tell of the things they saw and experienced, you will be disappointed. Many of those stories are incredible to hear, virtually impossible to argue with, and no doubt, point to the reality of there being life after death (we will deal more with this in chapter 2). I will not even be dealing with the theological implications and ramifications of such an event happening to someone. However, what I want to do is journey through the Scriptures, find those passages that tell us something about death and dying of the believer in Jesus Christ, honestly explore those passages, and then think about what these passages teach us about what happens to the believer when he or she steps inside the gate. I truly believe that we are going to be fascinated, encouraged, and comforted by what we uncover.

If you have ever wondered what happened to your loved one when he or she died, or ever think about yourself dying one day, then read on. While there is much that we will never know until we too experience this passing, I think there is much that we can learn and be assured of as we approach our own *miraculous moment* when we step inside the gate.

1

APPROACHING THE GATE

According to the Centers for Disease Control and Prevention, in the year 2020, there were 3,383,729 deaths in the United States of America.[1] Among those who died, 350,831 reportedly died from the COVID-19 virus that was beginning its sweep across our country.[2] Many of our loved ones were taken from us by this disease, as well as by heart disease, cancer, stroke, accidents, and other causes. These deaths left holes in relationships, vacancies in homes, loneliness in families, and unfinished plans, dreams, and hopes for those of us remaining.

When we think of such staggering numbers, we might be tempted to imagine nothing more than a herd of people being ushered out of the land of the living and on to who knows where. Death counts may become nothing more than statistics, except to those who lost a spouse, a father, a mother, a son, a daughter, or a dear friend. What about the person who died? To that person, just being numbered among the millions of others who died in 2020, or any other year for that matter, is cold and calculating. This brings us to a couple of haunting questions concerning death and dying.

This book is written primarily concerning the death of

---

[1] "Deaths and Mortality," Centers for Disease Control and Prevention, last modified September 6, 2022, https://www.cdc.gov/nchs/fastats/deaths.htm.

[2] "Deaths and Mortality."

◆ Dr. Danny L. Moody ◆

people who know God and are known by Him. Another volume could, and probably should be, written about what happens to those who die without a personal relationship with Jesus Christ. I assure you that it would not make for pleasurable reading.

Let us zero in on these two facets of the event of death in the life of the believer.

QUESTION ONE: "GOD, WHY DIDN'T YOU DO SOMETHING?"

The term *theology* simply means "a study of God." There is a theological term to describe one of the attributes of God, and that is the word *omniscient*. This simply means that God is all-knowing.

There is another word and characteristic of God, and that is the word *omnipotent*, meaning God is all-powerful. When you put these two attributes of God together, we come to understand that God knows everything and He can do anything.

What do these truths mean for us when it comes to the issue of death?

First, they let us know that the death of a believer does not catch God by surprise. In God's sovereign wisdom, He knows the exact time, place, and circumstances surrounding the homegoing of His child. God will not find out that you have died by reading it in the obituaries of your local newspaper.

Wise Solomon, in writing about the sovereign wisdom of God in Ecclesiastes 3:1–11, put it this way.

> To everything there is a season, and a time to every purpose under the heaven:
>
> A time to be born, and a time to die;
>
> A time to plant, and a time to pluck up that which is planted;
>
> A time to kill, and a time to heal;
>
> A time to break down, and a time to build up;
>
> A time to weep, and a time to laugh;
>
> A time to mourn, and a time to dance;
>
> A time to cast away stones, and a time to gather stones together;
>
> A time to embrace, and a time to refrain from embracing;
>
> A time to get, and a time to lose;
>
> A time to keep, and a time to cast away;

A time to rend, and a time to sew;

A time to keep silence, and a time to speak;

A time to love, and a time to hate;

A time of war, and a time of peace.

What profit hath he that worketh in that wherein he laboureth?

I have seen the travail, which God hath given to the sons of men to be exercised in it.

He hath made every thing beautiful in his time: also he hath set the world in their heart, so that no man can find out the work that God maketh from the beginning to the end.

Second, they let us know that the death of the believer was planned by God. King David, "a man after God's own heart," put it this way: "My times are in thy hand" (Psalm 31:15). The writer of the book of Hebrews makes it clear that the times of our deaths are a matter of record: "And as it is appointed unto men once to die, but after this the judgment" (Hebrews 10:27).

For every person God creates and places on earth, He has a divine purpose and plan. Within that plan, there is a starting point and a finishing point; conception is the starting point and death is the finishing point. When, in the plan of God, His servant has finished the course, and hopefully accomplished all that God has prescribed for him or her to do, God graciously calls an end to the journey by way of death.

Did you know that Moses also wrote songs? He did. One of the songs attributed to him is Psalm 90. It is about God's sovereignty and complete control over all that happens on earth, including our brief contributions to its history. Our stories are part of His story—history. Look at what He says about our lives.

For all our days are passed away in thy wrath:

> We spend our years as a tale that is told.
>
> The days of our years are threescore years and ten;
>
> And if by reason of strength they be fourscore years,
>
> Yet is their strength labour and sorrow;
>
> For it is soon cut off, and we fly away. (Psalm 90:9–10)

As the apostle Paul reached his own journey's end, he wrote to his young protégé, Timothy, these words.

> For I am now ready to be offered, and the time of my departure is at hand. I have fought a good fight, I have finished my course, I have kept the faith: Henceforth there is laid up for me a crown of righteousness, which the Lord, the righteous judge, shall give me at that day: and not to me only, but unto all them also that love his appearing. (2 Timothy 4:6–8)

When we combine the two attributes of God and focus on the death of His saint, we can know that in the *omniscience* of God, He knew it would happen, and in the *omnipotence* of God, He planned for it to happen. The will of God was done. Who could ask for anything more or less than for God's will to be done?

A word of caution and warning is worth noting here. Beware of those "Christian" teachers who would have you believe that you can somehow rebuke death or have faith enough to escape physical death. Both scripture and history have proven that no one is capable of such a feat. While it is true that the believer will live forever, it will not be exclusively in this world and not in this realm of existence. God has never intended that we live forever in this world, in these bodies, and with all the human frailties that we now know. We will deal more with this in chapter 3. It is through the avenue of death that God has chosen to conclude our earthly journeys and purposes and bring us home to be with Him.

If you have ever had the experience, as many of us have, of waiting on and giving care to one who is at death's door, knowing that the event is near and yet not knowing when it will happen, you will understand what I am about to say. These hours, days, and maybe even weeks, are totally, emotionally draining. It is like clamping booster cables to your body, but instead of pouring energy into you, they drain the energy from you. You don't complain, and you would do it all over again if you needed to, but it is an unexplainable and difficult way to pass the hours.

As a visual thinker, I like to think of it and describe it this way. Our loved ones are making their way along a path toward the gate—the gate into the presence of Jesus. We come alongside to join them on this journey. We walk, talk, and serve our precious ones to the very best of our abilities. The journey may be slow, exhausting, and thoroughly heart-wrenching. When we arrive at the gate, we stop. It is closed, and there is no latch on our side of this barrier between heaven and earth; it must be opened from within —in God's way and in God's timing. This is as far as we can go.

In many or perhaps most cases, I believe our loved ones are very aware of our presence, love, and grief. If they could, I am sure that they would express the most heartfelt thanks that they have ever expressed. We wait. We cannot see what is going on in the unseen world. We can see the eyes of our dear ones, but we cannot see what those eyes see.

They see the gate swing open, and quietly, in one final breath, they step inside the gate. This is a miraculous moment.

To answer the question that we started with—"God, why didn't You do something?"—He did! In His wisdom, He knew what was best; in His power, He did what was best. He always does what is best.

QUESTION TWO: "GOD, WHERE WERE YOU?"

Tragically, there are occasions when people get mad at God for taking their loved ones away from them. Their anger turns to bitterness, and their bitterness turns into a lifetime of misery as they spend their days shaking their fists at God.

If God was indeed a cold, distant, uncaring, and ruthless deity, who was only consumed with unrivaled authority and unrelenting domination, then perhaps such an attitude could be justified. However, this is not the God that we find revealed in the Bible. Quite the contrary! In passages that deal with the death of His children, we find a God who is not only aware, as we have just seen, but a God who is present and involved in gracious and gentle care and grace.

Let us start with one of the most noted and memorized passages of the Bible, Psalm 23. This song is sometimes called the "Shepherd Psalm" because of the way that it begins: "The Lord is my shepherd, I shall not want." The remainder of the song describes the way that our Shepherd, Jesus Christ, wisely and carefully guides our journeys through all of life's issues and complexities. One verse that stands out to us as we are thinking about the death and dying of the believer is verse 4.

> Yea, though I walk through the valley of the shadow of death, I will fear no evil: for thou art with me; Thy rod and thy staff they comfort me. (Psalm 23:4)

We have here a beautiful word-picture of a shepherd (Jesus Christ) leading his sheep (us) along a dark, unknown, and seemingly dangerous portion of the path. The sheep, vulnerable, defenseless, and no doubt fearful about what may happen to them, have reason to take pause. However, knowing that their wise, caring, and capable shepherd, is leading the way, their fears take flight and faith in the shepherd takes root.

The phrase "the shadow of death" comes from one Hebrew word *salmawet*, which means "death-shadow" or "to become dark; turn black." This word characterizes the world of the dead.[3]

One commentator described this image this way.

> The valley of the shadow of death—is a ravine overhung by high precipitous cliffs, filled with dense forests, and well calculated to inspire dread to the timid, and afford a covert to beasts of prey. While expressive of any great danger or cause of terror, it does not exclude the greatest of all, to which it is most popularly applied, and which its terms suggest.[4]

Death is scary unless you have a shepherd who knows the terrain, has defeated all possible dangerous enemies, and has Himself walked through this valley and came out *completely triumphant*. Jesus Christ has done that. He accompanies

---

[3] Francis Brown et al., "salmawet," in *The Abridged Brown-Driver-Briggs Hebrew and English Lexicon* (Boston Mass.; Houghton Mifflin Company; 1906), Logos Bible Software.

[4] Robert Jamieson et al., *Commentary Critical and Explanatory on the Whole Bible* (Oak Harbor, WA: Logos Research Systems, 1997), 1:354.

the believer as he or she comes to this dreaded part of the journey. With His "rod and staff" (tools of His trade as a shepherd), He confidently leads His sheep through a place that would be overwhelming and overpowering to anyone who does not enjoy the privilege of walking with Him.

One little girl missed the proper wording for the first verse of this psalm, but I think she captured the message when she misquoted it this way: "The Lord is my shepherd, that's all I want."

Pause for a moment and let that sink in. When our loved ones, or we ourselves, come to that *miraculous moment* of death, we have the promise of God, who cannot lie, that Jesus Christ will walk every step of the way through this process of dying. I am saying again, there is something *supernatural* that happens at this point of the journey.

Just a few months ago, at the time of this writing, my precious mom passed away at the age of ninety-one. My dad had gone to be with Jesus almost ten years earlier. Since that time, she had constantly prayed that God would just take her to heaven. In the last few months of her life, she struggled with one health issue after another, and it became apparent that her time on Earth was limited.

In the weeks and days before she passed, she struggled to do anything on her own and ultimately was confined to her bed. We brought in hospice help and we, the children, did everything we could to make her comfortable. After taking turns to care for her, on the night of her passing, my sister and brother were staying by her bedside. Her breathing was shallow and infrequent. She raised her head toward the ceiling and said one word - "Lord"—then lowered her head and was gone. It was a *miraculous moment* indeed.

Could it have been that she was seeing Jesus, as the Great Shepherd, coming to walk with her through the "valley of the shadow of death"? I think that is very likely what was happening.

Before we move along too far, and so I can gain some composure, I want to point out another Scripture dealing with this transitional period that we call death. In Luke's gospel, Jesus gives us the account of the rich man and Lazarus. Without going into detail, I want to point out a little tidbit of information in verse 22 that I find interesting. The "beggar" that Jesus refers to is Lazarus and this is what He says: "'And it came to pass, that the beggar died, and was carried by the angels into Abraham's bosom: the rich man also died, and was buried'" (Luke 16:22).

What I want to call your attention to is the phrase "was carried by the angels." This verse indicates that angelic beings are also involved in the transition into heaven. It could be that when the soul departs from the body (we will deal more with this in the next chapter), angels retrieve the soul and transport it into the presence of the Lord. Talk about a *supernatural escort.*

My overactive imagination kicks in here. I can almost see something like this: Jesus meets us at the gate, walks us all the way through the dark and scary valley, and on the other side are angels waiting for us. Jesus looks first at us, then motions for the angels to take a place on each side of us and says with a voice of victory, "Oh death, where is thy sting? Now, let's go home."

Another New Testament writer gives us a glimpse of the death of the believer. His name is Peter. You have to love Peter, right? So many of us can identify with him. He is writing to believers who are going through excruciating suffering, persecution, and great trials. In both of his letters, the key word is *suffering*, and the key issue is learning to trust God amidst the suffering.

Second Peter, chapter one, is one of my favorite chapters of the New Testament. It is full of great instruction and encouragement. I want to call attention to two verses in this chapter that relate to our subject.

> Wherefore the rather, brethren, give diligence to make your calling and election sure: for if ye do these things, ye shall never fall: For so an entrance shall be ministered unto you abundantly into the everlasting kingdom of our Lord and Saviour Jesus Christ. (2 Peter 1:10–11)

In verse 10, he charges these suffering believers to "make your calling and election sure." He is essentially saying, "Make sure you are saved." When that is settled, Peter assures his readers that they will experience what he calls an "entrance" into "the everlasting kingdom of our Lord and Savior Jesus Christ."

We have heard and used the phrase "making a grand entrance." Peter uses this same image when a follower of Jesus Christ, even one who has endured great suffering, steps through the gates and enters the presence and kingdom of Jesus Christ. When a child of God goes home, it makes news in Heaven.

Let me point out a phrase that Peter uses here, where the implication is not apparent in our English translations: "ministered unto you abundantly." The word *ministered* is a compound Greek word from *epichoregeo*, which means "to provide or supply." What is interesting, however, is that the root word is *choros*, which means "to dance." (My Baptist brethren are cringing here at just the mention of dancing.) The idea here, implied by the use of this word, is that when the believer enters heaven, there is a huge celebration of his or her arrival, and *abundantly* so.

The word *abundantly* is the Greek word *plousios,* which means "richly" or "with wealth." Some translations render it as "a rich welcome." Again, my overactive imagination engages, and I can see a welcoming into heaven, with hugs, shouts, applause, and probably even some dancing. I can't believe I just said that.

We can put to rest any presumption that when our saved loved one departs this life, he or she enters some kind of cold, silent, eerie, existence where people are floating on clouds and playing on harps in a minor key. No, there is a party going on, and he or she is an honored guest.

You know something? Death doesn't seem so scary anymore. No wonder the psalmist David wrote the short little verse, tucked inside his one hundred and sixteenth psalm, that says, "Precious in the sight of the LORD is the death of his saints" (Psalm 116:15). This word *precious* is a Hebrew word often used to describe jewels or precious stones. It indicates that, as God considers what is happening when one of his children is coming home, He beams with delight, as if beholding a diamond of great value.

If I might be so bold as to paraphrase what is being said here, God can't wait until we get there. God is smiling, His arms are open, as he welcomes his child home.

2

Far from Being the End

Merriam-Webster defines the word *transition* this way: "a change or shift from one state, subject, place, etc. to another."[5] A synonym, used here in this definition, is the word *change*. I might put it this way: the way things used to be is not the way they are now.

When I think about *change* and *transition*, there are several words that come to mind: scary, exciting, new, different, adaptation, and others.

In our world, change is not always welcomed. Someone has said, "The only people who appreciate change are babies." I think you know what I am talking about.

This is probably more information than you are interested in, but for Sherry (my wife of over forty-four years) and me, if my count is right, we have moved fourteen times over the course of our married life. However, we have lived only in the state of Texas. I have lived in only three counties in this state. Each move created change, but those changes were not extreme or life-altering for us. I guess this will be my testimony: "I am Texan born and Texan bred, and when I die, I will be Texan dead."

For the follower of Jesus, at the event of death, a transition or change occurs that is far more extreme and life-altering than anything that you or I have ever

---

[5] *Merriam-Webster*, s.v. "transition *(n.)*," accessed December 1, 2022, https://www.merriam-webster.com/dictionary/transition.

experienced. In the next chapter, we will be discussing some of these changes.

The Scriptures do not give us a lot of detail about what physically happens at the point of death. We do have information about the event of death, as well as where we will be after we die. Our task then is to logically put together the chronology of what happens when we die.

There are a couple of passages that helps us with this task.

> Therefore we are always confident, knowing that, whilst we are at home in the body, we are absent from the Lord: (For we walk by faith, not by sight:) We are confident, I say, and willing rather to be absent from the body, and to be present with the Lord. (2 Corinthians 5:6–8)

Without getting too technical here, Paul uses a present, active participle, translated "at home," and a present, active verb, translated "absent." This simply means that "at home in the body" (present and active) is a right-now state. When death happens, we become "absent" from the body (present and active) which is also a right-now state. Being "absent from the body" means that we are "present with the Lord." This is an immediate transition, from right now to right now. This fact becomes important a little later in our discussion.

Another passage comes from the words of Jesus mentioned in the previous chapter concerning the death of Lazarus, the beggar.

> "And it came to pass, that the beggar died, and was carried by the angels into Abraham's bosom." (Luke 16:22)

It is obvious that when Lazarus died, his body remained physically and visibly here on earth. However, notice that Jesus clearly explains that Lazarus himself was "carried by the angels into Abraham's bosom." How do you explain that the body of Lazarus is lying lifeless on earth, and yet Jesus says that Lazarus, himself, has transitioned to Abraham's bosom?

Both passages let us know that there is indeed life after death. This means there is more to our physical existence than merely the bodies that we live in. Available information such as this is what makes the Bible, God's Word, the most important piece of literature in all the world. Let's dig into this a little deeper.

The subject of death is an important issue in the collision of two diverse worldviews. Here is what I mean by that. An atheistic, secular worldview holds that there is simply no room for a belief in a spiritual realm. This means that the only "reality" is found in the things which can be seen; there is no spiritual dimension beyond the physical world. This worldview is called *physicalism*.

In the teachings of *physicalism*, there is obviously no room for the existence of a sovereign God. Life as we know it is the result of evolutionary process, and human life is nothing more than the physical bodies in which we live. Therefore, what might be called the consciousness or mind of a human is nothing more than the electrical impulses of the brain. When a person dies, the brain ceases to function, the body shuts down, and the person dies—nothing else, end of story, period.

There are obviously many unanswered questions within this belief. For instance, if human life is only the result of matter that has evolved, how and when did this matter achieve the ability to think, reason, feel, and act on its impulses? How can inanimate matter produce rational and emotional responses? In this worldview, even the ability to love, care, sympathize, and build relationships is nothing more than electro-induced functions of the brain. That seems sort of cold and flat, doesn't it?

However, we who hold to a biblical worldview firmly believe that there is a sovereign God, He is the Creator of all things (including humans), and that He is the sole source of life for all things. God is the designer, sustainer, and provider of all things in heaven and on earth. Information on Him and the work that He has done and continues to do is found in one place: the Bible.

What does the God of the Bible have to say about humankind and its existence?

God has created people to be more and possess more than just physical, visible bodies. He has created people not only with physical bodies but also with souls, invisible and yet very real parts of our essences. Listen to what happened even in the creation of the first person to ever live.

> And the LORD God formed man of the dust of the ground, and breathed into his nostrils the breath of life; and man became a living soul. (Genesis 2:7)

The forming of a human from the "dust of the earth" constituted the physical and the "breath of life" constituted the spiritual; therefore, "man became a living soul." The worldview that holds that a human being is both physical and spiritual is called *dualism*, the counterpart to *physicalism*.

In *dualism*, where the Bible is the foundation and authority, human consciousness is made possible not merely by the brain but also by the soul. Hundreds of times in Scripture, we find the Hebrew words *nephesh* (usually translated "soul"), *ruach* (usually translated "spirit"), and the Greek word *psyche* (usually translated "soul"). Biblically then, a human is a spirit/body dichotomy.

Lee Strobel has recently written an excellent book entitled *The Case for Heaven*. In relation to this subject of the human soul, he quotes J.P. Moreland, who says, "I am a soul, and I have a body."[6] This leads us to logically conclude that a soul can live and exist without a body, but a body cannot live and exist without a soul.

Jesus also pointed to this dichotomy of both body and soul.

> "And fear not them which kill the body, but are not able to kill the soul: but rather fear him which is able to destroy both soul and body in hell." (Matthew 10:28)

Here, Jesus clearly states that there is a definite existence and distinction between these two components of humankind.

Listen to the words with which Jesus assured the thief on the cross after the thief had put his trust in Him.

---

[6] J.P. Moreland, *The Soul* (Chicago, Ill: Moody Publishing, 2014), quoted in L. Strobel, *The Case of Heaven* (Grand Rapids, MI: Zondervan, 2021), 29.

And Jesus said unto him, "Verily I say unto thee, To day shalt thou be with me in paradise." (Luke 23:43)

The physical body of the thief was taken down from the cross after he died and was likely buried. However, Jesus assured him that on that day, he would still be very much alive and be with Him in paradise.

I know that I have gone to great lengths here in making a case for the dichotomy of humans, but this is very important as we come to what happens to a believer at the point of death. To know with certainty that there is life after death, just not in the physical body, is what gives us lasting hope. This hope applies not only to our loved ones who have already passed away, but also to all of us who will one day follow them.

At God's appointed time, unless Jesus returns beforehand, every believer will leave this world through death. At that moment, the soul/spirit of the individual departs the body and is immediately taken into the presence of Jesus (Philippians 1:20–23; 2 Corinthians 5:1–8). The body will remain to be buried or cremated. The soul then begins what we might call an intermediate state of existence in heaven with Christ. We call this an intermediate state because the soul has no physical body in which to dwell; it has had one in the past and will have one in the future, at the Resurrection, but just not now.

The apostle Paul gives a lengthy but vivid explanation of what is happening at death and points us to the future event of the Rapture/Resurrection in his letter to the Corinthians:

> But some man will say, How are the dead raised up? and with what body do they come? Thou fool, that which thou sowest is not quickened, except it die: And that which thou sowest, thou sowest not that body that shall be, but bare grain, it may chance of wheat, or of some other grain: But God giveth it a body as it hath pleased him, and to every seed his own body. All flesh is not the same flesh: but there is one kind of flesh of men, another flesh of beasts, another of fishes, and another of birds. There are also celestial bodies, and bodies terrestrial: but the glory of the celestial is one, and the glory of the terrestrial is another. There is one glory of the sun, and another glory of the moon, and another glory of the stars: for one star differeth from another star in glory. So also is the resurrection of the dead. It is sown in corruption; it is raised in incorruption: It

is sown in dishonour; it is raised in glory: it is sown in weakness; it is raised in power: It is sown a natural body; it is raised a spiritual body. There is a natural body, and there is a spiritual body. And so it is written, The first man Adam was made a living soul; the last Adam was made a quickening spirit. Howbeit that was not first which is spiritual, but that which is natural; and afterward that which is spiritual. The first man is of the earth, earthy: the second man is the Lord from heaven. As is the earthy, such are they also that are earthy: and as is the heavenly, such are they also that are heavenly. And as we have borne the image of the earthy, we shall also bear the image of the heavenly.

Now this I say, brethren, that flesh and blood cannot inherit the kingdom of God; neither doth corruption inherit incorruption. Behold, I shew you a mystery; We shall not all sleep, but we shall all be changed, In a moment, in the twinkling of an eye, at the last trump: for the trumpet shall sound, and the dead shall be raised incorruptible, and we shall be changed. For this corruptible must put on incorruption,

DR. DANNY L. MOODY

and this mortal must put on immortality. So when this corruptible shall have put on incorruption, and this mortal shall have put on immortality, then shall be brought to pass the saying that is written, Death is swallowed up in victory. O death, where is thy sting? O grave, where is thy victory? The sting of death is sin; and the strength of sin is the law. But thanks be to God, which giveth us the victory through our Lord Jesus Christ. Therefore, my beloved brethren, be ye stedfast, unmoveable, always abounding in the work of the Lord, forasmuch as ye know that your labour is not in vain in the Lord. (1 Corinthians 15:35–58)

Paul makes it clear that we cannot take our current, corruptible and mortal bodies into heaven with us, writing "flesh and blood cannot inherit the kingdom of God; neither doth corruption inherit corruption." The truth is, heaven would not be heaven if we were still encumbered by these old, sin-cursed bodies (we will speak more about this in the next chapter). Notice that he also points to the fact that while these bodies are laid aside for the time being, there will come a day when we receive new, glorified bodies, fit for holy and heavenly places, and that will take place at the Day of Resurrection.

Prior to and awaiting the time of the Day of Resurrection, the souls of the saints are in heaven with Jesus in this intermediate state.

Some scholars suggest that during this intermediate state, the soul, though certainly invisible now, may have some form of a temporary, spiritual body. This position is held because of what Paul mentions in 2 Corinthians 5:1–2.

> For we know that if our earthly house of this tabernacle were dissolved, we have a building of God, an house not made with hands, eternal in the heavens. For in this we groan, earnestly desiring to be clothed upon with our house which is from heaven.

Does the "building of God, an house not made with hands, eternal in the heavens" refer to the time-period immediately after death, in the soul state, or is it a reference to the glorified body? For me, the jury is still out on this question.

Another indication of a temporary, spiritual body of some kind during this intermediate state is that when departed saints were made visible to earthly inhabitants, they were clearly distinguishable. An example would be when Jesus carried Peter, James, and John up to what we call the Mount of Transfiguration in Matthew 17:1–6, they saw Moses and Elijah, who were recognizable.

Finally, over more than four decades of serving in ministry, I have stood beside the beds of many individuals in their last minutes before death. I have watched and heard as they called out the name of some loved one who had already passed away. They seemed to glimpse these departed loved ones, meaning their loved ones must have some kind of form that is recognizable and identifiable.

The bottom line is this: when the believer departs this life, the soul immediately goes into the presence of Jesus. The body is left, awaiting the Day of Resurrection and its eternal glorification. The departed loved one may have a temporary spiritual body. It may be that the soul, though invisible to our eyes now, will be visible in the spiritual world that it now inhabits.

There are some other questions that I think we would do well to address. First, what about the passages that refer to those who have passed away as being "asleep"? Does this not mean that they are totally unconscious and unaware of any kind of reality? The answer to this question is *no*. Some religious groups hold to the doctrinal position of "soul-sleep." This doctrine teaches that when a person dies, he or she is simply in a state of complete oblivion to existence, until the resurrection. At that time, the person comes back to life in a glorified body. The Scriptures pointing to the immediate transition of the soul into the presence of Jesus make it plain that there is consciousness, though in a soul-state, of those who have departed this life and gone home to be with the Lord. The reference to being "asleep" pertains only to the *physical body* of the departed one, because that body is indeed "resting" from realities of life until the day it is raised again by Jesus.

What about purgatory? There is a widely accepted teaching of a place called Purgatory, where departed ones go after death. Their sins are "purged" by fire until they are acceptable enough to enter heaven. The Greek word for "fire" is *pur* and thus the word purgatory, or "perfected by fire." The idea is that the amount of time spent in purgatory is dependent on how sinful the person was and how many prayers are being offered up on behalf of this individual by his or her survivors. I want to be clear on this: *there is no Scriptural support for this teaching.*

The passage usually cited in support of purgatory is found in 1 Corinthians 3:11–15.

> For other foundation can no man lay than that is laid, which is Jesus Christ. Now if any man build upon this foundation gold, silver, precious stones, wood, hay, stubble; Every man's work shall be made manifest: for the day shall declare it, because it shall be revealed by fire; and the fire shall try every man's work of what sort it is. If any man's work abide which

he hath built thereupon, he shall receive a reward. If any man's work shall be burned, he shall suffer loss: but he himself shall be saved; yet so as by fire.

The context of this passage itself makes clear that Paul is talking about those who are already saved. He is speaking about the "works" of the individual following his or her salvation. Notice this: the fire of judgment here is upon "works" and not "people." Truly, as believers, once we are saved, we should be working fervently for those things that are of eternal significance. For this, we will reap reward— gold, silver, and precious stones—from God for our service. It would be terrible to stand before Christ to give account of ourselves to Him, and have nothing of value to present, just wood, hay, and stubble.

Suffice it to say, *there is no biblical support for such teaching.* The price for *all* our sin has already been paid by Jesus Christ on the Cross. Our admittance into heaven is only possible by *what He has already done* and *our complete faith and trust in that work.*

There are others who teach that when an individual passes from this life, he or she ultimately returns to exist in this world in another form. This is called reincarnation. As with the previous arguments, *there is no biblical support for this teaching.* The writer of Hebrews makes clear that this one life is all that any of us have: "And as it is appointed unto men once to die, but after this the judgment" (Hebrews 9:27).

I come back to the word we started with in this chapter: *transition*. One day, we will transition from these earthly bodies, our souls will take flight into the very presence of Jesus, and that will happen at that *miraculous moment* of death, when we step inside the gate.

You know, one day I am going to leave Texas. My body may remain out there in Springhill Cemetery, but I will have moved. Then and only then will I be truly home.

3

THIS CHANGES EVERYTHING

There have been a few times in my adult life when I have driven into a car dealership in my old used jalopy and ended up driving away in a brand-new car. There were not many times, but there were a few. I must say, there is something exhilarating about that experience. The new car has no wear and tear, everything is tight and quiet, and there are no McDonald's french fries smashed into the carpet. The glass is spotlessly clean, and everywhere is *that new car smell*. I do not know what creates that smell, but it is intoxicating. I do know that you pay out the wazoo for it, but oh, what a smell! It is intoxicating—at least until that first payment comes due. My driving experiences are not nearly as dreadful in a new car as when I had to climb behind the wheel of an old rattletrap.

I can't help but snicker as I drive away, leaving that frustrating, tired and boring bucket of bolts on the parking lot of the dealership and thinking, *Just look at me now.*

I guess you know where I am going with this, right?

For our whole human existence, we have been stuck in the same old earth suits we call our bodies. We have had to feed them, fix them, and fuss over them. We have had to dress them, doctor them, and diet for them. We have had to wash them when they were dirty, mend them when they were broken, exercise them when they were becoming flabby, rest them when they became tired, and cosmetically enhance them when they started to show their age. They are the only ones we get down here, so we make the best of them.

The truth is that we cannot even completely wrap our minds around any kind of existence that does not include our flesh-and-bone habitation. Yet, when we look into the Scriptures, we find that for every person who lives on earth, there will come a time when life here ends, the flesh is vacated, and a very real existence begins in either heaven or hell. *This changes everything.*

In this writing, we are exploring what happens to the child of God at death. We are finding that a whole new world opens when he or she steps through the gates of heaven. As we learned in the previous chapter, death involves the separation of the physical, fleshly body from the spiritual soul of an individual. The soul then goes to heaven to be with Christ, where it will remain in an intermediate state, awaiting the resurrection of the dead when He, Jesus Christ, comes at the Rapture.

What is that like? What does it mean to be in a soul-state? What are our loved ones doing right now in heaven? Are they aware of what is going on earth? If you think that this subject creates a lot of questions, you are absolutely right. If you think that I am about to give you all the answers, you are absolutely wrong. I would if I could, but I honestly don't have them.

The apostle Paul provides a clear disclaimer for inquiring

minds like ours when it comes to what God has prepared for us: "But as it is written, Eye hath not seen, nor ear heard, neither have entered into the heart of man, the things which God hath prepared for them that love him" (1 Corinthians 2:9).

He tells us here that we have never seen, heard, or thought of anything like it. Our finite minds cannot comprehend an infinite domain. This is no doubt the reason that there is very little detail or description of our soul-state or intermediate existence in Scripture. If He told us, we couldn't grasp it. I think that even a mere glimpse of what heaven is really like would cause us to be so anxious to get there that we would be prone to do foolish things to expedite our departure from Earth. We would become, as the old saying goes, "so heavenly minded that we are no earthly good."

Paul records having such a glimpse into this heavenly realm, and he tells us that he heard "unspeakable" or "inexpressible" words, which are "not lawful" or "permitted" to even be told.

> It is not expedient for me doubtless to glory. I will come to visions and revelations of the Lord. I knew a man in Christ above fourteen years ago, (whether in the body, I cannot tell; or whether out of the body, I cannot tell: God

knoweth;) such an one caught up to the third heaven. And I knew such a man, (whether in the body, or out of the body, I cannot tell: God knoweth;) How that he was caught up into paradise, and heard unspeakable words, which it is not lawful for a man to utter. (2 Corinthians 12:1–4)

The "man" he is speaking about, is no doubt himself, as the text goes on to reveal. He asserts that this realm of life is beyond human description or vocabulary. His language here reminds me of what God told Isaiah some 700 years before the birth of Christ, and is certainly fitting for the place that God has prepared for those who love him when they die.

For my thoughts are not your thoughts, Neither are your ways my ways, saith the LORD. For as the heavens are higher than the earth, So are my ways higher than your ways, And my thoughts than your thoughts. (Isaiah 55:8–9)

With these disclaimers in mind, here is how we will need to explore, to the best of our abilities, what heaven in the intermediate state will mean. Since the flesh and fleshly issues are left behind, we can only surmise what it would be like to exist without those encumbrances. All we have ever known, and now know, is life in the flesh with its limitations, frustrations, and compulsions. These are the good, the bad, and the ugly of a physical existence. All of these are left on the parking lot of the dealership as we drive away.

Think with me for a little while about what an existence that is totally *free* from earthly and fleshly encumbrances will be like.

THERE WILL BE NO HEALTH ISSUES

The older I get, the greater this sounds. However, even in the prime of life, we have all experienced sickness, injuries, aches, and pains. Some individuals have never lived even one hour of life without the plague of these discomforts. Despite all our very best efforts to eat right, exercise, rest well, and protect ourselves, all we have ever known is the reality of a frail body that is susceptible to issues that we cannot control.

Think about this. When we go to heaven, there are no colds, coughs, cataracts, cavities, cancer, or casts. There are no headaches, heart attacks, hernias, hip replacements, or hot flashes. There are no bruises, bunions, bronchitis, bursitis, baldness, or bad breath. Thank You, Jesus! Get the picture?

In the great resurrection chapter of the New Testament, 1 Corinthians 15, Paul describes the ultimate glorification of the believer that will happen on the day of resurrection. However, in so doing, he gives us some vital information about the abandonment of our fleshly bodies, which happens at death.

> So also is the resurrection of the dead. It is sown in corruption; it is raised in incorruption: It is sown in dishonour; it is raised in glory: it is sown in weakness; it is raised in power: It is sown a natural body; it is raised a spiritual body. There is a natural body, and there is a spiritual body. And so it is written, The first man Adam was made a living soul; the last Adam was made a quickening spirit. Howbeit that was not first which is spiritual, but that which is natural; and afterward that which is spiritual. The first man is of the earth, earthy: the second man is the Lord from heaven. As is the earthy, such are they also that are earthy: and as is the heavenly, such are they also that are heavenly. And as we have borne the image of the earthy, we shall also bear the image of the heavenly. Now this I say, brethren, that flesh and blood cannot inherit the kingdom

of God; neither doth corruption inherit incorruption. (1 Corinthians 15:42–50)

In this passage, when referring to the present body that we live in, he uses words like *corruption, dishonor, weakness, natural,* and *earthly.* These are descriptive words of our flesh when it is "sown" or "buried" at death. This is the kind of body that we leave behind when we *step inside the gate.*

Every possible ailment or impairment of the human body that can inhibit or annoy us will be a thing of the past when we leave this "vail of flesh." The real you and me (our souls) will continue to live in a perfect place, in perfect health, in perfect peace, and with our perfect Savior. Would you agree with me that *this changes everything?*

If you have cared for a loved one who has had a prolonged illness or disease and has suffered greatly because of it, you can relate to a statement I have heard many times when that loved one goes to be with Jesus. That statement is this: "He/she is not suffering anymore." You can probably identify with another sentiment as well: "I would love to have (name of person) back, but not in the condition that he/she was in." Such assurance, coupled with the grace that God generously gives, is no doubt the strongest impetus we have to get through the grief that comes in a time like this.

If you can think of a day when you "never felt better" and then multiply that by a thousand, then you are getting close to what it will be like when you move to your heavenly home. Knowing this should keep us faithful to Christ in the present, and confident in Christ for the future.

> For to me to live is Christ, and to die is gain.
> But if I live in the flesh, this is the fruit of my labour: yet what I shall choose I wot not. For I am in a strait betwixt two, having a desire to depart, and to be with Christ; which is far better: Nevertheless to abide in the flesh is more needful for you. (Philippians 1:21–24)

THERE IS NO AGING

I like what my wife Sherry says about age: "Age is just a number, and mine is unlisted."

The older we get, the more we realize the complications that aging brings into our lives. It is interesting that when we were younger, we could not wait to get older, but when we get older, we wish we could go back to our younger years.

Let me remind us, however, that age and aging are purely physical and earthly issues. The count starts the day we were born and ends the day that we die. Death is the only cure for getting old.

How old will we be when we get to heaven? Some have

speculated that we will all be thirty-three years old, since that is how old Jesus was when he died. I am not sure that we can prove such a theory. I would submit that since age is purely physical and earthly, when we get to heaven, there will be no age at all. It simply will not exist. At that point, we will only be measured in terms that are eternal.

There will be no deterioration of our bodies. We will be *perfect*!

THERE WILL BE NO NEEDS

Think about this: we have never had one single day of life without a need of some kind. This is true of every person, from the time of conception to the oldest living individual. These old bodies that we live in are very high-maintenance.

I think it is virtually impossible to imagine an existence where physical needs no longer exist. The baby in the womb is totally dependent on the life-giving supply that comes from the mother's body. When that child enters the outside world, it does so with a list of needs that must be met immediately: air to breathe, nutrition, warmth, and a whole lot of tender loving care. Through the days, months, and years that follow, that list continues to grow. I would encourage you to stop and ponder all the things, both actual and superficial, that we need to maintain normal lives. Have I mentioned we are very high-maintenance?

Keeping this list in mind. I want to remind us that these needs all have one thing in common: they are all connected to and derived from existence in the flesh. The reason we need air is that the body demands oxygen. The reason we need food is that body demands nutrition. The reason we need exercise is that the body needs mobility to prevent atrophy. You get the idea. A fleshly existence, complete with all of its needs, is all we have ever known.

However, when we, at death, step out of these earthly bodies and step inside the gate of heaven, we leave this needy flesh behind. I say again, it is virtually impossible to imagine a life where physical needs no longer exist.

Let us take a few minutes to simply contemplate such a life.

WHAT ABOUT FOOD?

I can hear someone saying something like this: "Well, if we are not going to get to eat in heaven, I'm not sure I really want to go there."

I can also hear another rebutting, "What about the marriage supper of the Lamb?" Yes, there is that, as recorded in Revelation 19; however, that happens when we have new and glorified bodies after the Resurrection (more about this a little later).

We would be hard-pressed to make a case one way

or the other as to whether there will be food in heaven, while we live in this intermediate, soul state. The point is that we will not have a need for food to sustain a physical body. This means we will never be hungry. Think about this: if indeed God provides what we know of as food, it will be only for our enjoyment, not because we need it to exist. Someone reading this right now is having a hallelujah moment just thinking about such a prospect.

WHAT ABOUT SLEEP?

Exhaustion happens when the body is depleted of the energy needed to continue operation. The key word in this statement is "body." The solution to the problem of exhaustion, or at least being tired, is rest or sleep.

God, in His great wisdom when He created the earth in which we live, divided time into two parts: day and night (Genesis 1:3–5). The day, He made for work, and the night He made for rest. He even included an entire day, the Sabbath day of each week, to be a day for rest (Genesis 2:1–3). God, by His own design, created the physical world with the inclusion of sleep or rest. The key word in this statement is *physical*. A universal truth is this: *we get tired*.

Heaven is a very real place that is far beyond the physical creation we are now limited to. Think about this: there is no night there (Revelation 21:25 and 22:5). The bodies that used to give out on us have been discarded when we stepped through the gate, and we are liberated from having to recharge them. It seems obvious that we will not sleep, because we will never be tired. Great news! The old adage "I will sleep when I die" is not exactly true. Our souls, the real us, in heaven will be awake, alert, active, and never in need of a time to relax or refresh.

WHAT ABOUT CLOTHING?

According to one source, in 2021 in America, the average person spent about $161 a month on clothes. The average American family spent around $1,700 on clothes that year, according to the Bureau of Labor Statistics.[7] By the way, women spend 76 percent more than men: between $150 and $400 each month or $125,000 over the course of a lifetime.[8]

Obviously, clothing is an essential part of our list of needs, although most of us in America have an excessive

---

[7] Yakub Mohammad, "64 Powerful Money Spent on Clothing Statistics in 2021," Renolon, last updated August 8, 2022, https://www.renolon.com/global-money-spent-on-clothing-statistics/.

[8] Lauren Bowling, "How Much Should I Spend On Clothes? (+The 11 Tips I Use To Save)," Financial Best Life, accessed December 1, 2022, https://financialbestlife.com/how-much-should-i-spend-on-clothing/.

amount. Yet, how often do we stand at the closet door and complain, "I don't have a thing to wear."

Clothing is intrinsically tied to the physical body we live in. Does it fit? Is it in style? Will it keep me warm enough or cool enough? Is it modest enough? Does it make me look fat? There is certainly nothing wrong with this concern, but we can become obsessed with the question "How do I look?"

Think about this, when we are *absent from the body*, this is one less thing that we have to worry about. As a matter of fact, all the clothing we will need will be issued to us upon arrival.

> And when he had opened the fifth seal, I saw under the altar *the souls* of them that were slain for the word of God, and for the testimony which they held: And they cried with a loud voice, saying, How long, O Lord, holy and true, dost thou not judge and avenge our blood on them that dwell on the earth? *And white robes were given unto every one of them*; and it was said unto them, that they should rest yet for a little season, until their fellowservants also and their brethren, that should be killed as they were, should be fulfilled. (Revelation 6:9–11; emphasis mine)

I guarantee you we will be lookin' good in heaven.

WHAT ABOUT SEX?

Now I have your attention!

The sexual appetite that humans possess is a God-given, beautiful, and precious gift, and is to be satisfied *only* in accordance with the standards set forth in the Scriptures. It is sinful that humans have sought to compromise and corrupt that which God intends to be sacred.

> Marriage is honourable in all, and the bed
> undefiled: but whoremongers and adulterers
> God will judge. (Hebrews 13:4)

This passage, as well as many others that could be cited, make it clear that God's gift of intimacy is only honoring and acceptable to God when it is done between a man and a woman in a covenant-marriage relationship. Anything outside this relationship is *sin*. Biblically, the gift of God-honoring sex is for two primary purposes: procreation (birthing of children) and pleasure (physical bonding between a husband and wife).

> Now concerning the things whereof ye
> wrote unto me: It is good for a man not
> to touch a woman. Nevertheless, to avoid

fornication, let every man have his own wife, and let every woman have her own husband. Let the husband render unto the wife due benevolence: and likewise also the wife unto the husband. The wife hath not power of her own body, but the husband: and likewise also the husband hath not power of his own body, but the wife. Defraud ye not one the other, except it be with consent for a time, that ye may give yourselves to fasting and prayer; and come together again, that Satan tempt you not for your incontinency.(1 Corinthians 7:1–5)

I want you to note this: sexual needs are physical (with the body) and marriage is an earthly relationship. With that said, it makes sense that when we are no longer in physical bodies or in this earthly existence, then this need will no longer exist.

Jesus gave us a glimpse of this truth.

And Jesus answering said unto them, The children of this world marry, and are given in marriage: But they which shall be accounted worthy to obtain that world, and the resurrection from the dead, neither marry, nor are given in marriage: Neither can they die any more: for they are equal unto the angels; and are the children of God, being the children of the resurrection.(Matthew 20:34–36)

The bottom line is that when we go to heaven, we will no longer have the need for sexual fulfillment, because we will be far beyond such a need.

Author Randy Alcorn summed this up beautifully.

In heaven, there will be one marriage, not many. That marriage will be what earthly marriage symbolized and pointed to, the marriage of Christ to his bride [the church]. So we will all be married—but to Christ.[9]

WHAT ABOUT RELATIONSHIPS WITH OTHERS?

In our earthly existences, I would dare say that few, if any of us, would be able to function effectively if we had to live in absolute isolation from other people. Maybe a hermit, living off the land in the backwoods somewhere,

---

[9] Randy Alcorn, "Will There Be Marriage in Heaven?," Eternal Perspective Ministries, posted February 3,2010, www.epm.org/resources/2010/Feb/3/will-there-be-marriage-heaven.

could somehow manage, but not most us who might be considered "normal." We need one another.

However, with those relationships comes both the good and the ugly. Despite the many benefits of having others in our lives, relationships can also involve and include things like misunderstandings, confrontation, anger, hard feelings, and unforgiveness. This is true because we are presently living in sin-cursed flesh.

The need for relationships seems to be somewhat different from the other needs that we have been discussing. I think I would explain it in this way. In heaven, we will not need relationships with others because relationship with others is perfectly provided by everyone there. We will take none of our baggage from down here with us into heaven.

It is the soul of the person that is redeemed by the blood of Jesus Christ. It is the soul of the person that goes to be with Jesus Christ at death. When we pass into heaven, only the perfected parts of us will exist, and this will be true of every person there. That means that we do not have to fear coming across someone in heaven that we may have had problems with here on earth. We also do not have to fear getting into any scrapes or skirmishes with anyone there.

What a thought! The nasty and tragic divorce of two believers that happened down here is perfectly settled and past. That bitter wedge that seemed to exist between two former believing friends is gone and they are worshipping together side by side.

What a thought! Arguments never happen. Misunderstandings never happen, because now, we all understand perfectly. Everything that goes on happens in perfect peace. We are all the same race (the human race). We are all of the same denomination (blood-bought-believers). We are all of the same political party (King Jesus). We are all from the same backgrounds (sinners saved by grace). We all share the same desire (giving glory to the One Who sits on the Throne).

Let this truth circulate through your mind and heart for a few minutes: Heaven will be a place of sweet, pure, and unending fellowship with everyone there, especially Jesus.

There will be no time issues

Are you like me in this regard? Sometimes I dread going to bed at night because I know that in just a few hours, I must get up and go again. "I owe, I owe, so off to work I go!"

Schedules, appointments, deadlines, and responsibilities are a way of life for most people. Our lives generally consist of places to be, people to meet, and tasks to complete. Alarm clocks and reminders on our phones are necessary to make sure that we are where we need to be at the time we are supposed to be there. God forbid that we should miss an appointment or even be late.

Think about this. In heaven, there is only one measure of time: *eternity.*

Can you imagine the relief we will experience when we step beyond the gate, and *time* is a thing of the past? There will be no clocks on the walls, no watches on our wrists, and no cell phones in our pockets. There will be no calendars to update, no appointments to juggle, and no "Sorry I'm late" apologies to make. Sounds like heaven, doesn't it?

I wonder how long it will take us to relax and unwind upon arrival in that land where time has no meaning. Listen to what the psalmist wrote.

> For a thousand years in thy sight
> Are but as yesterday when it is past,
> And as a watch in the night. (Psalm 90:4)

The apostle Peter was referring to this passage when he wrote, "But, beloved, be not ignorant of this one thing, that one day is with the Lord as a thousand years, and a thousand years as one day" (2 Peter 3:8).

THERE WILL BE NO WORRIES

William Marshall, in his book *Eternity Shut in a Span,* uses this illustration.

For several years a woman had been having trouble getting to sleep at night because she feared burglars. One night her husband heard a noise in the house, so he went downstairs to investigate. When he got there, he did find a burglar. "Good evening," said the man of the house. "I am pleased to see you. Come upstairs and meet my wife. She has been waiting 10 years to meet you."[10]

It may not be burglars, but I think that most, if not all of us, would admit that we carry a constant load of something that occupies our minds in burdensome ways. My wife Sherry sometimes complains that when she goes to bed at night, "I can't turn my brain off!"

From the time we are old enough to process life until the time we draw our last breath, we have issues, responsibilities, concerns, and simple worldly weights in our minds and on our shoulders. One old boy put it this way: "When I don't have anything to worry about, I worry about that."

I have good news. It will not always be that way! The apostle Paul, a man who certainly knew about bearing burdens, points us to that future.

---

[10] William R. Marshall, *Eternity Shut in a Span* (New York: Pageant Press, 1959)

For which cause we faint not; but though our outward man perish, yet the inward man is renewed day by day. For our light affliction, which is but for a moment, worketh for us a far more exceeding and eternal weight of glory; While we look not at the things which are seen, but at the things which are not seen: for the things which are seen are temporal; but the things which are not seen are eternal. (2 Corinthians 4:16–18)

In Mark 4:19, Jesus mentioned what He called the "cares of this world."

And the cares of this world, and the deceitfulness of riches, and the lusts of other things entering in, choke the word, and it becometh unfruitful.

These cares are, as He is teaching, a huge distraction in life. However, notice that He calls them cares "of this world." For the children of God, when we step out of this world at death, and into the world of God's domain, the cares are left behind.

It makes sense to me that because we are living with perfect health, no needs, with perfected people, in a perfect land, and (the best part) in the very presence of God the

Father and God the Son, we can say in the words of the old hymn, "How beautiful heaven must be!"

Another question that I raised earlier is this. "Are the departed saints aware of what is going on here on earth?" The closest thing that we can come to a biblical answer is found in the book of Hebrews.

> Wherefore seeing we also are compassed about with so great a cloud of witnesses, let us lay aside every weight, and the sin which doth so easily beset us, and let us run with patience the race that is set before us. (Hebrews 12:1)

This verse describes the saints of God who have already departed this life, the "heroes of the faith" in chapter 11. It seems that the "cloud of witnesses" here is a reference to these departed ones and would obviously include all other departed as well. This verse indicates that they are "witnesses" to our existence here on earth.

However, based on all the other heavenly conditions that we have seen, it seems obvious that while they may well be seeing what is going on, their views and understanding of the events on earth will be far superior to earthly experience and emotions. Though impossible for us to fully understand, it seems that while they may observe events, they see past any anger, sadness, anything disconcerting, or that would hamper their heavenly happiness. On the other hand, our earthly joys, victories, accomplishments, and celebrations would add to their delights and may very well be fully enjoyed by our loved ones in heaven. Please keep in mind that this view, in answer to the question that has been asked, is only my logical but still speculative opinion.

By the way, do you remember that new car that I mentioned in the beginning of this chapter? Well, it is an old car now. It doesn't sound like it used to sound, look like it used to look, drive like it used to drive, and it certainly doesn't smell like it used to smell. That is okay. It will do. I am hopeful that it still has a few more miles left in it.

That sounds a lot like me. I have a few more rattles than I used to have, a few more dents that wrinkle my skin, my headlights don't shine as bright as they used to—you get the idea. That is okay. It will do. Hopefully I still have a few more miles left in me.

When I cross that finish line of life and go to be with my Jesus, well, friend, *that changes everything.*

4

FACE TO FACE

I t is likely that each of us has admired some individual from a distance but never had the opportunity to see, meet, and speak with that person. This may have been a celebrity, political figure, sports icon, or even a well-known spiritual leader. We know a lot about that person, are aware of the accomplishments that has made him or her famous, and would no doubt pay good money to get to meet, shake hands, and take a selfie with him or her. However, at least at this point, you have never met them face to face.

If and when you meet that person, it is common to experience a condition called being starstruck. You may experience sweaty palms, shortness of breath, and a stumbling tongue. You just can't believe that you are actually in that person's presence.

What about *Jesus*? Would He be on your bucket list of people you want to meet?

For most of you who are reading this book, you go to Sunday school and church to learn about Him and worship Him with fellow followers of Christ. You may have even joined Bible studies or enrolled in seminary courses to gain a better knowledge of who this Jesus is. Your spiritual journey through life is wrapped up in things pertaining to this man named Jesus.

If you are indeed a child of God, I can say without any successful contradiction that no one has done more for you than Him. He died for your salvation. He rose and ascended to heaven to make intercession for you. He has guided, comforted, strengthened, and a million other things that we may or may not realize.

His name is the most famous name on earth and has been for more than 2,000 years. His work of creation is what makes life—all life—possible. No one is more powerful, sovereign, compassionate, or glorious than He is. He is the "author and finisher of our faith." He is the "Alpha and Omega, the beginning and the end." With Him, "nothing shall be impossible." To each of us, He is a "friend that sticks closer than a brother." Yes sir! That is someone I want to meet—and I will one day.

We have looked at many aspects of departing this human life and stepping inside the gate. I am convinced, however, that the greatest facet of going to heaven when we die will be that we will see Jesus face to face. After all, He is the reason that we will be there.

There are two significant passages in the writings of the apostle Paul that let us know that seeing Jesus will be a reality.

> For to me to live is Christ, and to die is gain. But if I live in the flesh, this is the fruit of my labour: yet what I shall choose I wot not. For I am in a strait betwixt two, having a desire to depart, and to be with Christ; which is far

better: Nevertheless to abide in the flesh is more needful for you. (Philippians 1:21–24)

I love the words of verse 21: "to live is Christ, and to die is gain." These words make it clear that death is not the end of our existence—it only gets better. The words I want to point out, however, are found in verse 23: "to be with Christ." In this life, we are assured that Christ is with us *spiritually*. However, when we leave this life, we will be with Christ *physically*.

Just before His crucifixion, Jesus gave his disciples words of incredible encouragement, as recorded in John's gospel, chapters 14 through 16. He assured them that, despite His imminent departure to heaven, they would be with Him again. He told them in John 14:3, "'And if I go and prepare a place for you, I will come again, and receive you unto myself; that where I am, there ye may be also.'" The initial phase of the great promise begins at the point of death: "'where I am, there ye may be also.'" The mansions that He spoke of will come later; however, being in the presence of Jesus, according to the words of Paul, will be immediate when we depart from this life.

In this life, we enjoy being around people we love. The epitome of this kind of relationship and fellowship will be realized when we get to stand in the presence of Jesus Christ Himself and "to be with Christ."

The second passage that we need to consider is found in Paul's letter to the Corinthians.

> Therefore we are always confident, knowing that, whilst we are at home in the body, we are absent from the Lord: (For we walk by faith, not by sight:) We are confident, I say, and willing rather to be absent from the body, and to be present with the Lord. (2 Corinthians 5:6–8)

This passage points us to two definite locations of our existence. While still living in these human bodies, we are "absent" geographically from the Lord. In this state, our relationship with the Lord is "by faith, not by sight." However, when we vacate these bodies and are "absent from" the bodies, we are immediately in the presence of the Lord.

Paul uses a beautiful word here that I want to point out. The word translated "presence" is the Greek word *endemesai*, which literally means "to be at home."

The word comes from the root word *demos*, which means "popular assembly or people." The image is of a home-type environment with Jesus and with other people as a great big happy family. The idea that when we die, we float around on a cloud in outer space is far from valid. Can you imagine this? We will be present at an eternal family reunion (without all the complications that this may mean down here) and the patriarch of our family is none other than Jesus Christ.

I can imagine things like laughter, singing, praise, applause, thank yous, and celebration like we have never seen. All imperfections, altercations, ill feelings, suspicions, and strained relationships are things of the past. We are *one* with one another and *one* with Jesus Christ.

When I think of seeing Jesus in person, I am reminded of the occasion when Jesus carried three of His disciples up to the mountain that we call the Mount of Transfiguration. Here, Peter, James, and John had a glimpse of the person of Jesus in His glorified state. Listen to how Matthew describes the scene.

> And after six days Jesus taketh Peter, James, and John his brother, and bringeth them up into an high mountain apart, And was transfigured before them: and his face did shine as the sun, and his raiment was white as the light. (Matthew 17:1–2)

Notice that Matthew describes the face of Jesus as shining "as the sun." This speaks of the glory beaming forth from the countenance of the Lord. The glory is compared to that of the sun's brightness.

Mark is even more descriptive in relation to His garments.

> And after six days Jesus taketh with him Peter, and James, and John, and leadeth them up into an high mountain apart by themselves: and he was transfigured before them. And his raiment became shining, exceeding white as snow; so as no fuller on earth can white them. (Mark 9:2–3)

Mark shows us that the robe of Jesus was shining, white as snow, and incomparable to any human effort to create the whiteness it possessed. I give you this visual to suggest that this is likely the visual image we will behold when we see Jesus. The glory of Jesus will no doubt capture and hold our attention beyond anything else we may see in heaven. You want to talk about being starstruck? No one you have ever met can compare to the person of Jesus Christ.

In 1898, hymn writer and musician Grant Tullar received a group of poems written by Carrie Ellis Breck. Among these was one entitled "Face to Face." Tullar set the poem to music and it became one of the most popular hymns sung in Christian churches. Even though it is a little lengthy, I would encourage you to read every word of this old hymn.

Face to Face

Words by Carrie Ellis Breck and music by Grant Tullar

1. Face to face with Christ my Savior,
   Face to face—what will it be
   When with rapture I behold Him
   Jesus Christ who died for me?

   (chorus)
   Face to face I shall behold Him,
   Far beyond the starry sky;
   Face to face in all His glory,
   I shall see Him by and by!

2. Only faintly now I see Him
   With the darkened veil between,
   But a blessed day is coming
   When His glory shall be seen.

3. What rejoicing in His presence,
   When are banished grief and pain;
   When the crooked ways are straightened
   And the dark things shall be plain

4. Face to face—oh blissful moment!
   Face to face—to see and know;
   Face to face with my Redeemer,
   Jesus Christ who loves me so.[11]

---

[11] The Hymnal *for Worship & Celebration;* Nashville, Tennessee; Word
Music; pg. 549

5

THE RESURRECTION

Death is the end of life as we know it here on earth. As we have seen, however, death is not the end of our existence. According to the scriptures, as we have seen, our souls go to be with Christ in heaven in what we have termed an intermediate or soul-state. However, there is more to come than even this. Actually, there is much more than this, and if you can believe it, even more exciting than this.

In heaven right now, the souls of those who knew Jesus Christ as Savior are enjoying His incredible presence. We who now live and know Him will one day join them there if we pass from this life through the avenue of death. Those souls and those that will join them are waiting on the next great event in the scope of our eternity with the Lord: the Resurrection.

Listen closely to the encouraging words He gave the disciples, and ultimately to us, before the crucifixion.

> "Let not your heart be troubled: ye believe in God, believe also in me. In my Father's house are many mansions: if it were not so, I would have told you. I go to prepare a place for you. And if I go and prepare a place for you, I will come again, and receive you unto myself; that where I am, there ye may be also." (John 14:1–3)

Did you catch these four words "I will come again"? Jesus, now in heaven, with the souls of those who have departed, promises that He will return to the earth. He has never broken a promise, and He never will. *He will return.* I mentioned in the opening paragraph that those intermediate or soul-state individuals in heaven are "waiting." This is what they are waiting for.

The time when Jesus returns is unknown by any person or even the angels. Jesus said in Matthew 24:36, "'But of that day and hour knoweth no man, no not the angels of heaven, but my Father only.'" This is the event that we refer to as the Rapture is the next great event on God's timetable in relation to humankind.

There is much more information about this event and the events that will follow it in my previous book *Things to Come: Biblical Prophecy in Common Language.* Our focus here, however, is on the souls in heaven.

Again, the apostle Paul sheds light about how this will occur in relation to the departed loved ones in heaven.

> But I would not have you to be ignorant, brethren, concerning them which are asleep, that ye sorrow not, even as others which have no hope. For if we believe that Jesus died and rose again, even so them also which sleep in Jesus will God bring with him. For this we

say unto you by the word of the Lord, that we which are alive and remain unto the coming of the Lord shall not prevent them which are asleep. For the Lord himself shall descend from heaven with a shout, with the voice of the archangel, and with the trump of God: and the dead in Christ shall rise first: Then we which are alive and remain shall be caught up together with them in the clouds, to meet the Lord in the air: and so shall we ever be with the Lord. Wherefore comfort one another with these words. (1 Thessalonians 4:13–18)

The primary subject of this entire paragraph is the saved saints who have passed away prior to the Rapture. Paul's purpose is to assure and comfort those who remain alive. Follow along as we summarize this message of assurance.

- Notice in verse 13 that he is speaking about "them which are asleep." This would be departed loved ones who have gone to be with Christ. We may sorrow but we are not without hope.
- God will bring those who believe in the resurrected Savior with Him when He comes. That means that when Jesus returns, the souls of those in heaven will

accompany Him. They are waiting now, but one day their wait will be over.

- Note that in verses 15 and 16, we are told that those alive on earth will not *prevent* or "precede" those who come with Him. The "dead in Christ [who] shall rise first" are the bodies of these returning souls. These bodies will come forth from the earth, and as we will learn later, changed into glorified bodies. The souls will inhabit new bodies.

- The living believers will then be called up, changed, and glorified. At the same time, those souls returning with Christ will be united with their resurrected and glorified bodies and *so shall we ever be with the Lord.*

- Paul tells the grieving loved ones who are still living that this promise is their source of comfort; this is their hope, as well as ours.

I would never want to minimize the glory and splendor that our loved ones are experiencing right now in heaven. However, there is one incomplete facet to their existence: they do not have bodies.

Paul describes this incompletion to the Corinthians and assures them that full completion will occur.

For we know that if our earthly house of this tabernacle were dissolved, we have a building of God, an house not made with hands, eternal in the heavens. For in this we groan, earnestly desiring to be clothed upon with our house which is from heaven: If so be that being clothed we shall not be found naked. For we that are in this tabernacle do groan, being burdened: not for that we would be unclothed, but clothed upon, that mortality might be swallowed up of life. (2 Corinthians 5:1–4)

The "earthly house of this tabernacle" refers to our present bodies. If they dissolve or pass away, we have the promise of new, eternal, and heavenly bodies made by God. These would be the glorified bodies previously mentioned. His reference to being "naked" and later "unclothed" describe souls without bodies at all. We know this because he immediately continues by talking about being "absent from the body and present with the Lord." These souls desire that day when they are once again clothed with bodies–new bodies–through which "mortality might be swallowed up of life."

First Corinthians 15 is often called the Resurrection chapter of the New Testament. Paul begins the section by talking about the significance of Jesus's resurrection and ends by giving an exciting description of the resurrection of the saints. Look at what he says about the Resurrection and the new bodies that we will inhabit.

> Now this I say, brethren, that flesh and blood cannot inherit the kingdom of God; neither doth corruption inherit incorruption. Behold, I shew you a mystery; We shall not all sleep, but we shall all be changed, In a moment, in the twinkling of an eye, at the last trump: for the trumpet shall sound, and the dead shall be raised incorruptible, and we shall be changed. For this corruptible must put on incorruption, and this mortal must put on immortality. So when this corruptible shall have put on incorruption, and this mortal shall have put on immortality, then shall be brought to pass the saying that is written, Death is swallowed up in victory. O death, where is thy sting? O grave, where is thy victory? The sting of death is sin; and the strength of sin is the law. But thanks be to God, which giveth us the victory through our Lord Jesus Christ. Therefore, my beloved brethren, be ye stedfast, unmoveable, always abounding in the work of the Lord, forasmuch as ye know that your labour is not in vain in the Lord. (1 Corinthians 15:50–58)

Here, Paul clarifies that we cannot go into heaven in the bodies we now live in. These bodies are mortal and corruptible. At the resurrection of the saints though, all of this will change. The new bodies that we receive will be immortal and incorruptible. This will be the state, souls living in new and glorified bodies, that we will inhabit for all eternity.

Let me tell you just how glorious these new bodies will be. They will be like the resurrected and glorified body of Jesus Christ. Look at these passages.

> For our conversation is in heaven; from whence also we look for the Saviour, the Lord Jesus Christ: Who shall change our vile body, that it may be fashioned like unto his glorious body, according to the working whereby he is able even to subdue all things unto himself. (Philippians 3:20–21)

> Beloved, now are we the sons of God, and it doth not yet appear what we shall be: but we know that, when he shall appear, we shall be like him; for we shall see him as he is. (1 John 3:2)

Can you imagine a body like the body of Jesus? If you look at the gospel accounts Jesus's appearances before His ascension, you will find that He, in His glorified body, was not limited to time and space. He could appear and then disappear. He was visible and could be touched. He ate, spoke, walked, and best of all, was not tainted by the effects of the flesh and sin. We will be just like that.

The soul will no longer be naked or unclothed. It will be perfected, complete, holy, and in eternal communion with Jesus Christ. No wonder Paul told the Corinthians to "comfort one another with these words."

No, death is not the end. The intermediate-state is not the end. Living in a body like that of Jesus is where it all ends, and it can't get any better than that.

EPILOGUE

This place called Heaven is the destination of all who know Jesus Christ as Savior. It is, however, *only* for those who know Jesus Christ as Savior. Someone has said, "Heaven is a prepared place for a prepared people." Those who are not prepared go to a place the Bible calls Hell. As real as Heaven is, Hell is also real.

A prepared person is one who has received the free gift of salvation through Jesus Christ. Doing good, being baptized, going to church, and loving your neighbor are all good things and should be a part of your life once you know Christ. However, none of these can adequately prepare you for the day you die. Only a total faith in the death, burial, and resurrection of Jesus can do that.

Here is how you can be saved and know that when you die, you will also step inside the gate of Heaven.

1. Acknowledge that you have sinned against God, as all have.

For all have sinned, and come short of the glory of God. (Romans 3:23)

2. Admit that you cannot save yourself, as none can.

> For by grace are ye saved through faith; and that not of yourselves: it is the gift of God: Not of works, lest any man should boast. (Ephesians 2:8–9)

3. Believe with all your heart that Jesus died for your sins, was buried, and rose again that you might be saved, as He has indeed done.

> That if thou shalt confess with thy mouth the Lord Jesus, and shalt believe in thine heart that God hath raised him from the dead, thou shalt be saved. For with the heart man believeth unto righteousness; and with the mouth confession is made unto salvation. (Romans 10:9–10)

4. By faith, receive Him as your Lord and Savior, as He is seeking for you to do.

> But as many as received him, to them gave he power to become the sons of

God, even to them that believe on his
name. (John 1:12)

A sincere prayer like this has the power to save you and
give you a home in heaven when you die.

> Lord Jesus, I confess that I am a sinner and that
> I cannot save myself. I believe that you died
> on the cross for my sins, that you were buried
> and rose again the third day. Right here and
> right now, I ask you to forgive my sin, come
> into my heart and be *my savior.* In Jesus name
> I pray. Amen.

If you prayed that prayer and truly meant it, you are now
saved and prepared to go to Heaven when you die. You
will be eternally grateful for this moment in time when
you find yourself stepping inside the gate.

BIBLIOGRAPHY

Alcorn, Randy. "Will There Be Marriage in Heaven?" Eternal Perspective Ministries. Posted February 3, 2010. www.epm.org/resources/2010/Feb/3/will-there-be-marriage-heaven.

Bowling, Lauren. "How Much Should I Spend On Clothes? (+The 11 Tips I Use To Save)." Financial Best Life. Accessed December 1, 2022. https://financialbestlife.com/how-much-should-i-spend-on-clothing/.

Brown, Francis, Samuel Rolles Driver, and Charles Augustus Briggs. "Salmawet." In *The Abridged Brown-Driver-Briggs Hebrew and English Lexicon*. Place of publication: Publisher, Year of Publication.

"Deaths and Mortality." Centers for Disease Control and Prevention. Last modified September 6, 2022. https://www.cdc.gov/nchs/fastats/deaths.htm.

Jamieson, Robert, Andrew Robert Fausset, and David Brown. *Commentary Critical and Explanatory on the Whole Bible*. Vol. 1. Oak Harbor, WA: Logos Research Systems, 1997.

Marshall, William R. *Eternity Shut in a Span*. New York: Pageant Press, 1959.

Mohammad, Yakub. "64 Powerful Money Spent on Clothing Statistics in 2021." Renolon. Last updated August 8, 2022. https://www.renolon.com/global-money-spent-on-clothing-statistics/.

Moreland, J.P. *The Soul*. Original place of publication: Original Publisher, Original Publication Year. Quoted in L. Strobel, *The Case of Heaven*. Grand Rapids, MI: Zondervan, 2021.

THE FOLLOWING PAGES ARE INCLUDED
FOR YOU TO MAKE PERSONAL NOTES FROM
YOUR READING OR TO LEAVE MESSAGES
FOR YOUR FAMILY TO READ AFTER YOU
HAVE STEPPED INSIDE THE GATE.

Printed in the United States
by Baker & Taylor Publisher Services